Detachment Parenting

Detachment Parenting

33 ways to keep your cool when kids melt down

Heidi Smith Luedtke, Ph.D.

You Are Not Alone

As a mom of two small kids, I know how hard it can be to stay calm when the kids melt down. My own 25-pound 2-year-old can push all my hot buttons in less time than it takes to put breakfast on the table. Her older brother threw the mother of all hissy fits in our neighborhood supermarket...on Mother's Day. More than once I've felt like a failure as a mom because I said something snarky when I should have given my child a hug instead. If you feel like you're at your wits end, I promise you this: I've been where you are.

I'm lucky to have spent most of my professional life studying psychological research and techniques that address these challenges, and I've distilled key lessons in the detachment parenting approach. The strategies I describe in this book are designed to help you increase positive emotions, minimize stress, and stay engaged with your kids. When you use them in your everyday family interactions, you'll strike a balance between tending to feelings and taking action, what psychologists call emotion- and problem-focused coping.

Rest assured, detachment parenting is not the opposite of attachment parenting. It doesn't require you to deny your feelings, keep kids at arms' length or let them cry it out when they're distressed. That kind of disengagement couldn't possibly teach kids the emotion-regulation skills they need to be happy and healthy. Detachment parenting does not prescribe choices about how you feed, cuddle or care for your kids. Breastfeeding, baby-wearing, co-sleeping parents can use these techniques. So can bottle-feeding, stroller-pushing, sleep-scheduling parents. The detachment parenting approach rests solely on this core belief: Parents are best able to nurture and guide their children's development when they respond to kids' concerns with calm sensitivity, not frantic overwhelm.

I hope you put these techniques to work right away and that the skills you build help you achieve the level-headed, loving parenting style you want. Please reach out and share your successes. I'd love to hear how *Detachment Parenting* helped you realize more peaceful, productive interactions with your kids.

You can learn more about my work, read current articles, or submit questions or comments on my website, www.HeidiLuedtke.com. I'd be happy to answer your questions on my blog, where you—and others—can get inspiration, insight and support. We're in this together.

About This Book

Detachment Parenting will show you how to:

- Stay calm when kids are out of control
- Engage kids in helpful discussions of intense emotional issues
- Coach kids to understand and manage their own moods
- Be confident that you can handle emotional crises, and
- Feel better about yourself as a person and as a parent

In this book, you'll access the same self- and relationship-regulation strategies child development experts use to preserve a level-headed, nurturing demeanor, and learn to apply them in your own home.

Emotions are contagious; we catch them from our kids. And when that happens, it's easy to overreact. Detachment parenting is a mindset and a skillset. It allows you to break out of fight-or-flight mode and cues your body's natural relaxation response. After you regain composure, you'll find ways to revise your thinking so you can move forward effectively. You'll also learn how to build your child's mood-management skills. On the level, loving foundation you create for your family, you can all grow up together.

In *Detachment Parenting*, I present 33 strategies, organized into five sections:

In the Heat of the Moment offers practical tips for keeping your cool when you feel the adrenalin rush of fear, frustration or anger. These ideas prevent you from acting out when you're likely to lose it emotionally.

Addressing Kids' Concerns shows you how to interact with kids when their feelings are revved up. You'll learn how to listen, and what to say. These ideas keep you focused on coaching your kids through the mood-management process, so you don't get sidetracked by your own thoughts or feelings.

Seeing the Bigger Picture describes ways to step back mentally so you can see situational triggers and relationship patterns that make meltdowns more common and more destructive. With a broader view, you'll be able to prevent many crises before they happen and respond to challenges with greater composure.

Household Mood Maintenance describes ways you can build up reserves of emotional energy each and every day. These ideas will decrease frustration and friction for you and the kids, so you're all less likely to slip into meltdown mode. Happy habits you build now will stay with your kids forever.

Nurturing Your Own Well-Being suggests ways to treat yourself with care and compassion. These techniques help you get connected, savor simple pleasures, and revise negative thoughts so you feel affirmed and supported as a parent. Tending to your own emotional health ensures you have more to give the ones you love.

The examples in this book are aimed at parents of children from birth to age 6, but the underlying principles apply to kids (and parents) of any age. Feel free to tweak the techniques to make them fit your family and adjust your approach as kids grow. Detachment parenting is a flexible skillset you can use in any situation.

Contents

Introduction

Have you ever wondered how teachers, counselors and coaches keep calm when kids get out of control? You may think they are blessed with easygoing personalities or joke that they go home at night and drink themselves silly. In fact, most teachers and counselors do their jobs day after day without falling into self-destructive coping patterns. That's because they have learned how to dial down their own emotional responses and stay focused on guiding kids' learning, no matter what.

If you morph into "bad mommy" when you are overwhelmed, you're not alone. It's immensely hard to keep your cool when you have little personal or psychological space of your own. Grown-up pursuits—like work, hobbies and adult conversation—can't save your sanity when they are constantly interrupted by whiney demands, sibling squabbles and temper tantrums. Even stable, happy moms may snap under the pressure sometimes.

This book is packed with 33 detachment strategies you can use right away. It starts with simple ways to change course in the heat of the moment, when you're about to lose your cool. Once you've reclaimed calm, you'll learn how to stimulate and guide emotional discussions so kids feel valued and validated. Mental strategies for seeing the bigger picture will reveal emotional triggers and response patterns, and help you respond mindfully, without overreacting. You'll get tips for maintaining a healthy emotional climate each day and learn how to preserve and increase your emotional energy reserves so you can give more of yourself and feel more fulfilled.

With practice, you'll stop the vicious cycle of bad feelings, angry actions, and self-blame that is repeated each time you get stressed out. Detachment parenting principles will help you create a positive environment that minimizes big blow-ups and maximizes engagement and growth. You'll learn to control your feelings and to coach kids through challenging situations. Tackling heated issues as a family team will bring you closer together and reinforce the deep, loving bond you all share. You'll all experience more joy and less stress, and that will make you feel better about yourself as a parent and as a person. You may feel a little like Supermom. Really.

In the Heat of the Moment

*Read this section for ways to keep your cool when
fear, frustration or anger get you revved up.*

1. Count to 100

When you feel the initial inklings of anger, stop right where
you are and start counting. Silently or out loud, slowly count
from 1 to 100.

Make it fun and keep it slow by counting "1 alligator, 2 alligator…" or customize the countdown with your own special
word or phrase. Do not react to the emotion-inducing event or
situation until after you've reached 100.

Your emotion system is designed to work quickly—the chemicals that turn on the body's fight-or-flight response flood the
bloodstream in seconds, then dissipate almost as fast. Counting
fills up the time when you're most likely to overreact and come

out swinging. It allows you to delay your response until the initial surge of emotion subsides, without having to think of a stall tactic and without locking yourself in the master bedroom closet.

It's possible you'll be out of the danger zone after only 30 or 60 seconds, but don't rush to action. Keep counting—or put other measures in place—to avoid reacting before you are ready to think and to act rationally.

You may feel silly counting aloud. Do it anyway. Counting out loud models this technique for your kids and distracts them (in a silly way) from whatever drama came before. By countdown's end, both you and your kids will be ready to move in a different (and happier) direction.

2. Breathe

Belly breathing is easy to do, and it relaxes your body and tells your brain to calm down. Practice this technique before you need it, so you can use it without too much thought when stress amps you up.

Put one hand on your belly, just below your ribs, and lay your other hand on your chest. Take a deep breath in through your nose, and imagine the air is filling your belly. Let your expanding belly push your hand out. Your chest should not move if you're doing this correctly.

Blow out through mostly closed lips, as if you were whistling. Contract your belly to push the air out completely. You can use your hand to push the breath out if it helps you stay focused on using your abdomen. Repeat slowly, 5 to 10 times.

Rapid, shallow breathing is a common feature of the fight-or-flight response to stress. Slow, deep breaths activate the body's relaxation response instead. By tuning in to your breathing, you take the focus off external events that may be causing your distress and re-center yourself. Breathing is an easy and effective way to turn off the stress hormones that excite your body and brain, so you can think clearly.

If you have trouble slowing your breathing, count to 4 as you inhale, then count to 7 as you exhale. Under stress, you're likely to breathe in quickly and to breathe out only partially. Counting to 7 on the exhale will slow you down and ensure you empty your lungs before inhaling again. Once you are calm, you'll be able to choose a productive response to the situation.

3. Slow your Tempo

Your body's fight-or-flight response system gets your muscles ready to rumble and that can speed up your actions and words in ways you may not even notice. Pretend you're the star of a video drama and set the speed to slow motion. Deliberately slow down your movements and the pace of your words. A sudden burst of slow sucks the life out of the emotional storm that might have been swirling around you.

Slowing down breaks you out of an automatic pattern of responding. You'll feel more capable and in-control when you move and speak slowly. You'll also turn off the unintended signals you may be sending to kids that show them you are frustrated, angry or impatient. By turning off those signals, you prevent your own emotions from magnifying kids' distress. With a patient, metered approach you can discuss what's happening in a way kids understand.

Your unique temporal personality affects how you interact with kids even when there isn't a crisis at hand. The speed that feels good to you may be much faster or slower than your kids prefer. And the more rushed you feel to get things done, the slower kids may seem to act. Accept individual differences. Trying to get kids to march to the tune of your internal drummer will only lead to inefficiency and frustration. Build in extra time kids might need to get tasks done without feeling hurried or harassed. A slower pace may be the fastest way to regain and preserve your composure.

4. Change your Tone

Emotional distress does crazy things to your tone of voice. Some people shriek in a higher-than-usual tone. Others bark orders in a low grumbly growl. Tune in to your tone. Dial down the volume and speak in a mid-range tone, not too shrill and not too aggressive. Aim to speak in a clear, practical tone of voice, as if you are giving directions to a driver who is lost in your neighborhood. An easy-going but authoritative tone can instantly change the dynamic of an emotional situation.

When you lower the decibel level and strike a positive tone, you'll instantly reassert control over your behavior and help yourself to calm down. Others will be able to listen to what you say, without being distracted by the emotional cues in your voice. And rest assured: changing your tone doesn't necessarily mean changing your tune. Sometimes parents have to make unpopular statements, like "No, you can't have ice cream for breakfast." Imagine you are a customer service agent for a five-star luxury hotel chain. Deliver bad news with grace and poise, even if your kids threaten to pack their bags.

If you are struggling to find an even tone of voice, opt for a cartoonish tone instead. Sometimes the best way to learn a new skill is to exaggerate it until you get the hang of it. No one will be able to hold onto negative feelings when you're doing your best Bugs Bunny voiceover.

5. Take a Time Out

The point of a time out is to give yourself an opportunity to settle down and sort through negative feelings without escalating the conflict at hand. Tell your kids "Mommy needs a time out," and follow the rules you've established for kids' time outs. Sit in a designated spot. Don't talk to anyone. Don't play with your smart phone. Don't move. Just sit quietly and simmer down.

How long you sit out is up to you—let kids' ages (not yours) set the time limit. Small kids will not be able to fend for themselves if you take a 30-minute hiatus from hands-on parenting. When time is up, apologize (if necessary), give hugs all around, and move forward.

Most kids are familiar with the time out strategy, and they know the rules of the game. If your kids associate time out with punishment or abandonment, it's helpful to show them you can sideline yourself voluntarily. Doing so gives you an opportunity to collect your thoughts and prevents anxiety or anger from escalating.

If your kids are anything like mine, they won't be able to leave you alone during time out. Set a kitchen timer to keep track of the time: when the bell tolls, the kids know that mom's back in action. If they interrupt your time out, minimize your interactions, and keep a positive tone. You want to make time out look like an attractive mood-management strategy so the kids will follow your lead. You've hit the sweet spot when the kids start initiating their own time outs.

6. Switch Things Up

A complete change of context can help you circumvent feelings of frustration instead of acting on them. When the kids can't agree on who gets to play with the coveted electric "Thomas the Tank Engine" figure, redirect the action outdoors. Present the new activity in a fun way; don't threaten or make it a punishment by saying, "Since you can't share the trains, neither of you gets to play with them." Just change tasks swiftly and skillfully.

Say, "I've got an idea! Let's draw a family pictogram in the driveway for Daddy to see when he gets here!" Then grab the sidewalk chalk and head for the door. I promise: the kids will follow you.

Both parents and kids may need to get physical distance from their current situation to break out of the emotional pattern they're in. But kids probably don't have the ability to shift their focus without some adult intervention. Distraction is a healthy, short-term emotion-regulation strategy that works for both you and the kids.

You may worry that distraction lets kids off the hook when they ought to be disciplined, or that it reinforces a short attention span. The truth is people can't always solve problems in the heat of the moment. Switch-tasking gives everyone a brief reprieve so they can regroup and reconnect. You can reflect on the situation later, when everyone has moved past their distress.

7. Tag Team

There will certainly be times when the kids are on your last nerve and you just can't keep your cool. Call in reinforcements.

A spouse, friend or family member can step in and diffuse the situation while you get away and regroup. You don't have to be dramatic about asking for assistance. Look your partner in the eye and say "You're it!" in a way he'll understand. Then walk away before you blow up. Sequester yourself in the bathroom or go outside to get the mail. Shut (but don't slam) the door behind you to symbolize your disengagement from whatever is happening.

Moms often feel like we carry the entire burden of childrearing on our shoulders, even though partners, friends and family members love our children and want to contribute. Tapping out doesn't mean you are weak or inadequate. Accepting a helpful reprieve makes you a more centered and effective role model. Kids need to learn that everyone needs help now and then. Parents who ask for and accept assistance show kids it is okay to reach out to others.

If you've convinced yourself there is no one to call in a crisis, sit down and make a list. Now. In the margins if you must. Put your parents, siblings, best girlfriend, close neighbor, co-parent and partner on the list. Knowing you have people in your corner dramatically reduces the pressure that fuels mommy melt downs.

8. Ask for Empathy

Sometimes there's no one to tag. And you may have to ask your kids for support. When you're feeling down or on-edge, mention it to make kids aware. Say "Mommy's feeling grouchy today," or "I'm sad that my best friend moved away." Let kids know what they can do to help you feel better—maybe you'd like to spend quiet time watching TV together. Maybe you could use a good belly laugh. Describing fragile feelings and emotional needs helps you avoid potential problems before they arise. It also models self-regulation skills for your kids.

Whether you notice or not, your emotions affect everyone. Even infants can sense a parent's emotional state: It charges the air with negative energy. Kids may be scared they'll set you off and may misbehave because they feel bad but don't understand why. While your kids can't (and shouldn't) act like your therapists, they can (and should) feel they can talk to you about feelings, including yours. Sharing your feelings and asking for what you need re-affirms your responsibility for managing your own mood and gives kids permission to talk about what might be bothering you.

Beware of asking kids to just leave you alone. Detachment parenting is not the same thing as escapism, and it's not a good idea to be physically present but emotionally unavailable. When you really need time away from the kids, call for back up or pay a sitter.

Section One Recap

When you feel you are about to meltdown, shout, or react badly to your kids' behavior, respond with one of these techniques:

- Count to 100
- Breathe
- Slow your tempo
- Change your tone
- Take a time out
- Switch things up
- Tag team
- Ask for empathy

Any one of these strategies will keep you from overreacting—you don't have to remember them all. Choose a favorite from the list and use it when your emotions begin to swirl out of control. Using the same technique each time helps you build a habitual, calm response.

Addressing Kids' Concerns

*Read this section to learn how to interact with kids
when emotions run high.*

9. Be Present

If you quickly feel frustrated or distressed when kids' feelings flare, your automatic reaction may be avoidance. You may declare you're busy, walk away, or avoid eye contact to keep from catching kids' bad feelings. After a brief cool-down period—using a strategy covered in the previous section—it's time to get your head in the game. Kids' distress grows when parents don't listen. That means the more distance you seek, the more intensely kids will pursue you. They'll follow you, cling, and cry or complain until they get the attention they need.

When your child comes to you with a tearful or hostile expression, use this three-step strategy to be present in mind, body and spirit.

- STOP right where you are. Discontinue activities—the dishes or laundry or email can wait a few minutes.
- DROP to your child's eye level, so you can offer physical (not just emotional) solace.
- FOCUS on exactly what your child is feeling, and don't worry (yet) about why she is feeling that way. Go toward the emotional pain and take it all in, like a giant human sponge. Use soothing sounds, a big hug and nods of understanding to absorb your child's feelings.

Stop, drop and focus makes you a compassionate witness to kids' feelings and breaks the cycle of distance and pursuit that develops when one person avoids and the other seeks attention. It gives kids a sense of acceptance, love and validation, and those qualities provide the inner strength kids need when times are tough. Emotions level off, instead of growing more and more intense.

10. Talk Less

If you usually respond to kids' distress with interpretations and instructions, make a concerted effort to conserve your words. Giving advice and correcting kids' behavior adds fuel to the fire. Put a word limit on your response and use your words wisely.

Kids need time to feel, think and express themselves without interrupting or talking over their parents. Pay full attention to your child's report of what happened and emotional expressions.

Encourage her to continue talking by asking "Is there more?" when her story seems to stall.

Pause between statements and after you ask a question, count-ing (silently) to 10 each time. You may think you are giving kids time to respond when you aren't. Nervous energy may cause you to fill the silence with your own running commentary, so kids can't get a word in.

Listening is a powerful way to diffuse kids' distress and it allows you to keep your distance emotionally. But be careful to stay tuned in, rather than letting your mind wander to other ideas. (Mirroring, covered in strategy 13, can help you stay focused.) Once kids get a chance to fully express themselves, they're often ready to move on—even though the original problem remains unsolved.

If you find it challenging to be quiet, focus on using your body language rather than spoken language. Make eye contact. Nod in agreement or to show that you're following what your child is telling you. Keep your arms open and relaxed, so you send warm, welcoming signals instead of cold or critical ones. There are lots of ways to communicate without saying much out loud.

11. Label Emotions

Use your (limited) words to help kids develop a rich and nuanced vocabulary for expressing their emotions. Infants and toddlers can use sign language to express basic emotion concepts, such as happy and sad. Older children should know more specific labels for feelings, including:

- Happy
- Sad
- Angry
- Frustrated
- Scared
- Surprised

Temper tantrums are most common in kids who don't yet have the verbal skills to express their feelings. Labeling gives kids a way to make their point without clinging, crying or throwing a fit. But emotion words aren't learned by accident. Kids need to hear parents put emotion labels into appropriate context.

Studies show labeling emotions decreases activity in the emotional parts of the brain and increases activity in the regions responsible for coping and decision making. Differentiating between different negative states also breaks the anger-aggression cycle, and allows kids to handle angry feelings without resorting to hitting, spitting or biting. Labeling your own feelings is equally important.

Be careful not to confuse emotion labels with character judgments. Say "You seem really angry" not "You're acting like a jerk" or "You're being a brat!" Your goal in labeling is to increase kids' communication and self-regulation skills, not to diminish or disrespect their feelings.

12. Ask Questions

Let's face it: You're the one who changed his diapers, cut up his food, and kissed his boo-boos. You've been your kid's personal problem solver since the minute he was born. It's hard to break out of the doer role and accept a consulting role, but that's what detached parents do. One way to act like a consultant—even if you're itching to step in and fix things yourself—is to ask questions instead of making statements.

The best questions are neutral and child-focused. Use them to guide your child through the coping process without doing the work for him. Here's a quick question cheat-sheet you can adapt to almost any situation.

- What happened?
- Is there more?
- What could you do to fix things?
- Do you need any help from me?
- How did that work out?

The question method provides structure to your conversation with your child, and makes you more of a coach and less of a cop.

How would you feel if—at the end of a play date—you approached your mom crying big, alligator tears, and got this response: "There's nothing to cry about. I told you we had to leave in 5 minutes. Tell Jeffrey 'thank you' and let's go home."

(Lousy, right?) Imagine how much better it would be if your mom said: "Why are you so sad?" and waited for a reply.

It may take more time to ask than to tell, but in the long run, coaching is more effective than controlling kids' behavior. Answering questions helps kids understand their feelings and learn how to manage them. It reminds you (and your kids) that each of us is responsible for choosing how we act. And that helps everyone get along better.

Consistent use of the question method will teach your child how to coach himself through challenging situations. He will find he can ask himself the same series of questions you would ask, to guide his own thinking and behavior. Self-coaching is powerful tool for development in childhood and throughout life. Repetition is the best way to internalize these questions.

13. Reflect Feelings

Imagine your child says, "I am so mad at you! I wanted the big cookie and you gave it to Emma! You always give her the best stuff." (If your kids are younger, they may not say this in so many words, but I'll bet they express the same sentiment in other ways, including stomping, kicking, and pouting.)

What's your knee-jerk response? Most parents resort to denial, self-defense or a moral platitude like, "No one said life would be fair."

Here's the problem: These responses beg kids to keep arguing. That's not what you want. A counseling technique called mirroring is more likely to decrease frustration. Here's how you do it.

Listen to your child's words, and—as closely as possible—repeat them back in an empathic voice. Say, "It sounds like you're really mad at me because I gave Emma the big cookie. You feel like she always gets better stuff." Then pause and listen. Mirror the statements you hear. Don't fight back or be flippant. Just repeat your child's words with as little interpretation as possible.

Therapists use mirroring to allow clients to hear what they themselves are saying in a different way. Detachment comes as an added bonus. Mirroring helps you keep your emotions in check because it prevents you from inserting your own ideas. You're less likely to judge kids' feelings or take them personally if you're focused on reflection. And that means your child sets the pace. He will feel heard and accepted, and you won't have to soothe his hurt feelings with a bigger cookie or trumped up apology. If he suggests solutions, you'll be listening.

When he hears his words repeated back, your child may realize his original statement wasn't true, or that what he said wasn't what he meant. Allow your child to revise his original words and be patient while he works through his feelings and decides on a way forward.

14. Share Your Stories

You don't have to keep your own thoughts on the down low in order to maintain detachment. Think of your personal stories as the basis for the most important life lessons your child will learn. Share the story of how you lost your favorite stuffed animal. Tell your daughter about the summer when your best friend moved to Idaho two weeks before your dog died. Let kids know you feel angry when someone cuts in front of you at the gas pump. Use your stories as teaching tools, and explain how you felt, what you did, and how the situation worked out.

My son asks me to repeat the story of how I learned to ride a bike each time he gets on his own two-wheeler. I tell him about how my dad put training wheels on the bike, and how he held the handlebars steady as he pushed me down the street. I recall feeling scared and excited. My son listens with rapt attention, because the story resonates with his own experience.

Sharing personal examples levels the playing field and shows kids that grown-ups have problems and feelings just like they do. Stories help kids understand that their experiences are normal and that they can grow from their mistakes instead of letting bad feelings drag them down. Stories can send the "If I did it, you can, too" message loud and clear.

Stories can also help parents teach emotion skills (like listening, patience, and compromise) without being high and mighty. Because you're focused on your experiences, kids can step back from their feelings and move past them. When you want to connect with your child and help him detach from today's emotional triggers at the same time, tell tales.

The best teaching tools may have a similar theme to the child's present situation (for instance, loss, disappointment, making mistakes, being left out, sharing, or shyness) but have different details. For instance, if your daughter is terribly anxious about going to preschool, you may choose to tell her a story about the time you started ballet lessons and were so nervous you wouldn't get out of the car. A story that has too much overlap with her own situation might hit too close to home. Aim for a balance of similarity and uniqueness to give your child a chance to get perspective.

15. Buy Time

Even after your child shares her feelings and offers potential solutions, you may need time to think things through. For instance, your child might be upset that he can't attend a birthday party on Saturday because it conflicts with his soccer game. He may beg and plead to attend the party instead of going to his game.

It's okay to delay responding. Tell your child, "I'm not sure how I feel about that. Let me think about it and get back to you." Minimize your child's frustration by putting a time limit on the delay. Say, "I'll let you know my decision after dinner" or

"I'll let you know my decision when the clock says 12." Delaying the decision allows you to diffuse a volatile situation and makes it less likely you'll regret your response later on.

Buying time is a useful relationship-saving strategy. Studies show people can adjust decisions for feelings and biases, but doing so takes time. You are likely to over-correct for your biases if you respond when tensions run high. You might snap and say "You made a commitment to the team, and that's the end of it!" before you have a chance to think about how you'll feel if your child misses the birthday party. Issues that seem crystal clear in the heat of the moment often look different once you take a step back.

Hold yourself accountable to making a timely decision. Kids will quickly call your bluff if you say, "I need time to think about that" when what you really mean is, "I'm going to drag this out until you forget about it." And make sure everyone knows what you decided, even if they won't be happy about the outcome. Dodging kids' concerns will only increase their frustration.

16. Stay Positive

Negative words may creep into your vocabulary when you're upset or angry, and you may not notice it is happening. But your kids will. When the red "check engine" light comes on in the car and the pharmacy takes 48 minutes to fill your birth control prescription, you may fret out loud over how much it will cost to get the car fixed—if it's actually broken—and speak harshly and impatiently about the fact that you'll be late for piano lessons. The kids will pick up on your impatience and may act bratty because your anger makes them anxious.

The emotion system is designed to focus your attention on problems that need to be addressed, so it's normal to pay more attention to negative things than to positive ones. Tune in to the subtle effect of frustration. Your negative mindset might cause you to overreact to kids' whining or to their fidgeting in the drugstore checkout line. Pretty soon, everyone is feeling edgy.

As much as possible, highlight benefits, advantages, and opportunities that come from even the worst situations. Be unsinkingly optimistic. Cling to—and exaggerate—hope. Sell the silver lining. Things may not magically improve because you shout "Leaping lizards!" when your usual response would be "Dammit!" but you'll be in a better mental state if you preserve a positive outlook.

Positive words and a can-do attitude prime your brain to retrieve other positive information. You will see possibilities and opportunities where you would otherwise see limitations and challenges. Staying positive also brings out the best in people around you, so everyone gets in on the happy, upward spiral.

If you tend to be critical or pessimistic, you may find it challenging to channel Pollyanna. Start with neutral statements and work your way up. "That's interesting," "Oh my!" and "Let's see..." are my go-to phrases when the kids are over the edge and it looks like I might jump off the cliff right behind them. Intentionally seeking the bright side of a bad situation is a healthy mood-management strategy. Let your kids learn it by observation.

Section Two Recap

Giving in to whining or tantrums leads to more whining and more tantrums. Use these detachment parenting techniques to seize teachable moments and build kids' emotion-management skills:

- Be Present
- Talk Less
- Label Emotions
- Ask Questions
- Reflect Feelings
- Share Your Stories
- Buy Time
- Stay Positive

These techniques diffuse the current crisis and help kids understand, describe and handle their feelings. Combine them to create an emotional consultation strategy that suits your style and addresses kids' concerns.

Seeing the Bigger Picture

Read this section for ways to step back mentally so you can spot (and circumvent) emotional triggers and patterns.

17. Study the Situation

Imagine you're at the park and a nearby toddler cries out because another kid threw sand in his face. You might think "He's crying very loudly," or "He was surprised by that sand." You might look around to see whether the child's mother was rushing to the rescue. You might see the startled child pick up a handful of ammo and hurl it in the direction of his playmate.

If it's your own child, the situation is different. Crying calls you into action and instantly puts you in the mom spotlight. Other parents hear your child's screams, and they may judge your response to the crisis. You may feel you have to swoop in and save your child or prevent her from fighting back.

Intense emotions and past experience with your kids can color your response.

As often as possible, sit near your child and watch:

- What your child is doing or saying
- How your child is doing it (speed, order, tone of voice, body language, actions)
- How long the behavior persists
- How often it occurs

Focus on actions, and resist making assumptions about your child's intentions or motives. Notice patterns and cycles of behavior. What does your child do first? What happens next? Does the same action-reaction get repeated? Consider the situational context and what's happening in your child's relationships with other people. Jot down observations if that helps you stay focused on watching, not reacting.

Playing scientist can help focus in on what your kids do, rather than what you think or feel about their behavior. Observation may reveal your child's emotional triggers and response patterns. It can also help you stay calm when kids are out of control. Next time your child is throwing a tantrum in the aisle at Target, step back briefly and watch like a scientist observing a chimpanzee. You may find the whole event is much less emotional when you study the situation before stepping in.

18. Clarify Ownership

Because emotions seep into the air around us, it's easy to lose sight of whose feelings you're feeling. Your self-talk may be part of the problem. Do you catch yourself making statements like these?

- "I can't make anyone happy."
- "Everyone is watching my kid throw a fit."
- "Why do I have to do everything?"

If so, you may need to remind yourself that kids' concerns and emotions belong to them, not you. Shift ownership back to your kids with simple statements like these.

- "Emily is feeling angry."
- "Emily is struggling with this transition."
- "Emily needs help with her temper."

Repeat kid-focused statements like a mantra if you must. It's essential that you stay clear about which experiences and feelings are yours, and which experiences and feelings belong to your kids.

Giving kids ownership of their experiences and feelings puts you in a position to guide your child through a crisis, rather than fixing problems that aren't yours to fix. The bottom line is this: You can't make kids' feelings go away, even if you take them upon yourself. What you can do is teach your child emotion-regulation skills. Clarifying ownership of feelings allows you to stay focused on what your child needs.

Kids sometimes take parents' emotions personally. For instance, your son might jump into an argument you are having with your spouse and try to defend you by saying "You're being mean to Mommy!" or by hitting or kicking your spouse. If this happens, acknowledge your child's good intentions and take responsibility for handling the situation. Use "I feel" statements such as "I feel angry" or "I feel sad" to model ownership and teach emotion concepts. Give your child permission to detach from your emotions and take care of himself.

19. Lower your Expectations

It's easy to lose sight of behavioral milestones once your baby reaches the solid-food, walking-and-talking and potty-trained stage. You may be treating your child like a little adult, expecting her to sit still through hour-long restaurant meals or share favorite toys with complete strangers at the park. Reset your sights—lower. Read books, blogs and websites that describe normal behavior for children the same age as yours. Seek feedback from your child's pre-school teacher or from parents in your play group. Take your child's experience and personality into account and be realistic about what you expect.

Parents often overestimate what kids can do at their stage of development, especially if a child is precocious in other areas. My 2-year-old speaks in complete sentences—her verbal skills are on par with most 3- and 4-year-olds. But it wouldn't be fair for me to expect that she also has the self-regulation skills of an older child. Just this morning she bit her brother while he was eating his cereal. That is classic 2-year-old behavior.

Expecting too much sets everyone up for frustration, including you. Adjust your standards downward to meet your child where she is right now, and raise them as she grows and develops. What parents call bratty behavior is often completely age-appropriate. Consider whether your kids' actions may be a sign that you're asking them to do more than they can do at their current stage of development.

Remember to express your expectations in positive words, so kids don't feel incompetent or criticized. Say "Please pet the dog gently," instead of, "Don't pull the dog's ears!" Say, "Use nice words with your brother," instead of, "Watch your mouth!" Your kids will live up to your hopeful expectations.

20. Let Go of Outcomes

Imagine you are a tour guide, taking your child through the rainforest. You hope to show him the flora and fauna, and protect him from flooding or poisonous snakes. You design the tour so your child has amazing opportunities. But you can't control the weather and you can't be sure he'll see a sloth.

The emotional landscape is equally uncontrollable. You can't prevent every disappointment or make kids happy all the time, but you may still have trouble letting go. Parents feel an enormous sense of responsibility for kids' well-being. If you recognize your need for control is causing you to be uptight and (ultimately) unhappy, you may need to release the reins. Here are three ways to do it:

Visualize a role reversal. In your mind's eye, picture yourself as a frazzled tour guide. You are weighed down by unfolded, unwieldy maps, a compass, stopwatch, binoculars, and detailed itinerary. You fight against these objects as you try to paddle a canoe upstream to your destination. The kids whine about bugs, thirst and being bored.

Feel the pressure of trying to control everything for everyone. Then, see a shift. Picture yourself as a tour guide aboard a boat that is gently pulled down the chocolate river in Willie Wonka's factory. Watch with curious attention as your children see the Oompa-Loompas for the first time. Laugh as your youngest child tries to blow a bubble bigger than her head.

Feel the pleasure of sharing new and unexpected experiences. Hold on to this sense of detached wonder as you guide your kids through real life.

Exhale. Trying to control outcomes increases physical tension. You may have taut muscles, shallow breathing, and a narrow focus of attention. Let go of the physical tension by extending your exhalations. Consciously release all the controlling energy you have inside as you blow out each breath. Say, "Ahhh."

Emphasize effort. Do your best to handle each parenting challenge with grace and skill. Allow for do-overs, second chances, and repeat performances. When you look back at your development as a parent, you'll see you've come a long way since they were babies.

Section Three Recap

Increase your mental distance from trigger events and kids' feelings with these techniques:

- Study the situation
- Clarify ownership
- Lower your expectations
- Let go of outcomes

These strategies help you see how things can spiral out of control. With a bigger picture in mind, you'll be able to foresee potential problems and prevent them altogether. If crises arise, you'll respond with greater thoughtfulness and composure.

Household Mood
Maintenance

Read this section for practical ways to decrease friction and increase contentment for your entire family.

21. Follow Family Rules

A teacher would never dream of starting the school year without a written list of class rules prominently posted on the wall, and smart parents adopt the same strategy. Focus on three to five specific rules that apply to all family members, kids and adults alike. Phrase them in positive terms; "Don't yell!" is not the same as "Use your inside voice." Emphasize what you want instead of highlighting what you don't want.

Written guidelines can be read and reiterated to establish clear expectations and remind kids of the rules when they fail to act appropriately. Written rules improve your ability to keep a level head when kids misbehave, because the rules are external and impersonal. Parents set kids up for success when we're clear about what we expect from them.

The rules aren't about you (or your kids), they're about behavior. Focusing on actions helps everyone keep their emotional distance.

Older kids can collaborate with you to come up with rules and write them on poster board. Hold a family meeting to discuss ideas and agree upon rules that everyone can live with. Here are some examples to spur your thinking:

- Walk and talk quietly
- Listen carefully
- Keep your hands, feet, tongue and teeth to yourself
- Respect personal space and belongings
- Say please and thank you to each other
- Get and give hugs every day

Rules like these encourage everyone to be kind and respectful.

22. Embrace Routine

Waking up, getting dressed, eating breakfast and getting out the door to play group or school shouldn't be a major source of stress. Create a daily plan to accomplish necessary tasks with as little friction as possible. Write down the order of events and post it where you (and the kids) can see it. Make concepts easy for nonreaders to grasp using pictures to stand in for words. A toothbrush, clothes, food items, play toys and a bus might represent your morning plan. Put times next to the pictures so kids learn to associate clock time with tasks. A dinner plate, television, bathtub, pajamas, toothbrush, books and bed might capture your wind-down routine.

Refer to the task list whenever household events take an unexpected turn. Predictability decreases stress. Getting back on track restores a feeling of centeredness.

Self-sufficiency is an important goal for kids. Although there are times when it's wise to put kids in control, everyday chores aren't the best time to do it. Imagine their response if you ask your kids "Do you want to brush your teeth or read a book first?" That's right. They'll pick the book. And when you're done reading, they'll ask for another one.

The answer to "Are you ready to go to bed?" is "No." Always.

When it comes to required tasks, it's best to stick to a schedule. A structured plan allows kids to anticipate what will come next and to prepare for transitions. Try not to deviate until everyone gets the hang of the schedule. After that, you can flex a bit as needed. If you've made an impact, kids will remind you when you skip a step.

Routines may seem simple, but they have extraordinary power. Doing the same tasks in the same order each day enables you (and your kids) to accomplish more with less stress. When behavior becomes automatic, your brain is freed up to think about interesting ideas, like how to redecorate the master bedroom and whether it's worth it to switch cell phone companies (again). Show kids how a quick step-by-step strategy can streamline the most hectic times of day, and you'll give them an enormous gift. Schedules help us maintain self-discipline and stay focused.

It helps if your family routine is followed by everyone, including your partner. Don't create a plan so intricate that others find it stressful or nitpicky. Family members shouldn't need a stopwatch to stay on schedule. Aim for a simple, practical plan.

23. Move It (So You Don't Lose It)

Negative emotions stir up a lot of physical energy. Find a healthy outlet for it. Take a walk around the block, make silly faces, or get kids involved in a game of leapfrog. Put on an exercise video. Boogie around the living room to the latest Kidz Bop CD or the pop music channel that comes with your cable TV package. It's impossible to stay angry when you're all singing "Party Rock is in the House Tonight" at the top of your lungs.

Channeling your adrenalin-fueled energy into a heart-pounding activity lets you release tension and express feelings in a positive way. Your muscles warm up and feel-good chemicals called endorphins flood your body, making it hard to remember why you felt bad to begin with. Your brain gets extra oxygen and nutrients, and that brightens your mood and facilitates smart thinking. And the biological benefits persist even after you stop moving.

Putting fun moves on the daily schedule can help you get through tough times with the kids. At my house, the time between 4 p.m. and 7 p.m. passes painfully slowly. The kids are tired, but their little kid bodies are filled with restless energy. I am exhausted and feeling a little low, especially if I haven't heard from my husband all day. Rockin' out to the kids' latest favorite song (even if we're dancing to "Rudolph the Red-Nosed Reindeer" in June) puts us all in a good mood and lets everyone burn off extra energy before bed time.

If a dance party keeps you from reaching for cookies and ice cream to get through the afternoon slump, so much the better.

24. Reinforce Desired Behavior

Toward the end of the day, facilitate a conversation with your kids about what they did, what they learned, and how you all got along.

Discuss emotional episodes and put them in perspective, without assigning blame. For instance, you might say, "Wow! You sure were mad when your sister knocked down the Lego tower you built." Then compliment your child for what he did right (such as treating his sister with gentleness) and distill the lesson learned: "You worked hard to be kind even though you were angry. That's a hard thing to do." Add a brief suggestion about how to do even better next time, but don't lecture or punish. This is a time to open up dialogue and reinforce desired behavior.

Knowing that you'll have time to discuss emotion-related situations later reduces the pressure you feel to make things right immediately by hitting kids over the head with a reprimand or a lesson. You'll have a more productive conversation after everyone has time to cool off, and a play-by-play re-enactment is much less likely. Delayed discussion is also less likely to amplify kids' distress. Getting some temporal distance on the event gives everyone a clearer view and facilitates kids' learning at a time when they're more open to it.

It is okay to share your own experiences—especially if your kids are too young to carry a conversation—but don't make this talk about you. The day-end wrap-up gives kids a chance to make sense of what went on. You might talk every night over dinner or have a brief chat at bedtime. Soon, kids will start to look forward to sharing their thoughts.

End your discussion by asking kids what they're most excited about doing or learning tomorrow. Boost their anticipation by describing the very best parts of what is to come. Tomorrow's fun can be today's happy ending.

25. Practice Gratitude

As often as possible, write down good things so you will remember them. Include simple pleasures like the sound of your toddler splashing in the bathtub and the smell of fresh-baked banana bread. Jot down special treats, such as taking a day off from work or winning a prize or a contest. Include good things that are out of sight but close to your heart, such as your grandma in Florida and your best childhood friend's new baby. Keep account in a journal or fill a blessings box grateful statements scribbled on slips of paper. How you do it doesn't matter. Just do it.

Studies show each of us has a personal emotional set point. Negative events might cause our moods to get worse for a while, but they return relatively quickly to the usual level. The same thing happens for good events. The surge of joy subsides rather quickly, then we're back to situation normal, all stressed out. The good news is this: Research shows keeping a gratitude journal can actually reset your emotional thermostat.

There's an immediate mood lift when you count your blessings, and the lift lasts for months and months. The daily practice of gratitude teaches you to look for what is right, rather than what is wrong. It gives you a storehouse of positive memories to revisit when you feel down. And things you focus on grow over time, as you notice more examples and begin to cultivate happy moments.

There are lots of ways you can coach your kids to adopt a grateful attitude. When your child comes to you with a success story—like drawing a picture he's proud of or getting to be the class helper that day—ask, "What was the very best part?" Intentionally shifting kids' attention to positive features of a situation teaches a valuable self-regulation strategy.

At day's end, no matter what happened, play the "3 Good Things" game with each child. Take turns sharing three things you're thankful for and bask in your blessings. Gratitude is an attitude anyone can catch. Let your kids see you being grateful and they will learn to be grateful themselves.

Section Four Recap

Consistent attention to the emotional climate in your home can minimize meltdowns. These simple solutions help you create a predictable, positive environment every day.

- Follow family rules
- Embrace routine
- Move it
- Reinforce desired behavior
- Practice gratitude

Make mood-maintenance strategies a consistent part of your daily life. These happy habits will sustain you when times are tough and stick with your kids when they are all grown up.

Nurturing Your Own Well-Being

Read this section to learn how to tend to your own emotional health by seeking support, staying centered, and cultivating self-compassion.

26. Find a Village

Parenting young children can be isolating, even lonely, especially for stay-at-home moms. You don't have a group of colleagues to commiserate with when challenges get the best of you—and your partner probably isn't interested in a play-by-play recap of last night's sleep struggles. So join an online parenting site and swap stories with other moms. Seek out a local moms' group. Create a mom-friendly book or cooking club with several gal pals. Ask a couple of other moms to join you and your kids for a romp at the park after the library story hour. Do whatever it takes to make connections with other people whose interests (and issues) match yours. When problems arise, phone a friend.

Check out these mom-friendly orgs:

- Moms Club International
- Meetup.com
- Moms Club Worldwide Directory
- Café Mom
- Circle of Moms
- University of Moms
- Mothers of Preschoolers
- Moms' Support Groups
- Moms' Groups by Birth Dates at Babycenter.com and Babyzone.com and Parents Magazine
- Support For Working Moms at workitmom.com and meetup.com
- National Organization for Mothers of Twins Clubs

Talking with other moms helps to normalize the surreal moments in motherhood, so you don't start to think that you're losing your mind. It gives you a chance to be a grown up and to share what you know with people who might actually want to hear it. If you've got one good friend you can turn to, you'll preserve an adult perspective even when the situation is starting to evoke your best 5th-grade-girl behavior. A shoulder to lean on can keep you from turning kids into confidants, which would not be healthy for them or for you.

In a village, everyone shares responsibility and reaps rewards. Don't join a group in body and hold back in spirit. Social support is a two-way street. Be willing to put yourself (and your stuff) out there for others to know. It's not easy to find honest, compassionate peers, but you definitely won't find them if you're guarded or aloof. Make an effort to be personable and to get personal.

27. Make "Me" Time and Space

Motherhood is a 24/7 job, and it helps to take regular breaks. I know it's challenging to preserve some time for yourself. Be creative. Swap babysitting with a friend or neighbor so you can both get some down time once a week. The kids will get a play date and you'll each get a break: it's a win-win-win. Spend your protected time on things that matter to you, instead of catching up on laundry or picking up kids' prescriptions. Take a class at the local community college. Go for a long run. Browse your favorite store.

If you really can't get away from the house, wake up early or stay up late to spend half an hour on yourself. Read a book or surf the web without listening for fighting, crying or the eerie sound of silence that undoubtedly means your toddler is painting the walls with peanut butter.

It's also important for moms to make space for themselves in their own homes. I know that sounds silly. It's your house. You decorate, organize and clean it. You are responsible for making the house a home. But I daresay most moms don't have even one little corner to themselves. The kids type letters on your computer, take baths in your tub, and hide out under the clothes in your closet. They creep into your room at night and snuggle into the bed. You may start to feel claustrophobic or out of place in your own home. Make some space for yourself. Turn a closet into a computer station or scrapbooking center. Or designate one corner of the basement as your "mom zone." Post a sign to stake your claim. Physical boundaries create psychological space.

You give up a lot of free time and real estate when you become a parent. Of course, you gain a lot, too. Making time and space for yourself ensures your emotional energy tank stays above empty, and keeps you from growing short-tempered, resentful and bitter. It also helps you to stay present when you are with the kids, because you know you'll have mommy time later. Without the promise of time for yourself, you may try to multi-task kids' needs and your own. That can leave everyone (including you) feeling slighted.

28. Treat Yourself

Modern American culture seems to support the idea that true love (and therefore motherhood) is completely selfless. But denying your own wants and needs day after day isn't healthy. Constant giving without getting anything in return makes people feel disconnected from their own desires, and that disconnection creates resentment over time. Small, daily treats remind you that you are worthy of the same care you give to others. They prevent you from operating in deprivation mode, and that lets you feel calm and centered when life gets crazy.

Gather special objects into a designated "comfort drawer" you can raid when you need a pick me up. Imagine your comfort drawer is the grown-up equivalent of the travel kit you stock to keep kids happy while they're riding cross-country in the backseat of your minivan. Stash away small sweet treats, like candy-covered nuts. Add fancy tea bags, and bottles of scented bubble bath or luxurious moisturizer. Include treats for your eyes and your mind, like favorite photos and books of poetry, scripture or inspiring quotes. These tiny tokens will be your sanity savers when the day feels like a road trip through the desert with no water in sight.

When you feel deprived, you're more likely to let little things bother you. Treat yourself regularly so you don't start to feel unloved or unimportant.

- Download your new favorite song to your iPod.
- Buy yourself a charming bracelet.
- Take time to make a hot breakfast for yourself instead of grabbing a protein bar.
- Tape a favorite photo or inspiring message on your dashboard.
- Subscribe to a magazine filled with gorgeous images or irresistible gossip.
- Call a friend for no reason except to chat.
- Get a pedicure.

Building your reserves ensures you always have plenty of good feelings to give away.

29. Meditate

A number of meditation techniques, including guided imagery, mindfulness, Transcendental Meditation (TM), breathing- and heart-focused meditation have stress-busting benefits. If you already practice one of these techniques, set aside time each day to do it. If you aren't committed to a specific method, I'd recommend starting with a simple relaxation exercise like this:

- Sit or lie in a comfortable position.
- Leave your arms and legs straight and loose.
- Dial down distractions, like background noise and bright light.
- Breathe deeply to begin. Repeat 3 to 5 times.
- Next, progressively tighten and release the major muscle groups in your upper body.
- Begin by tightening the muscles in your forehead, mouth and jaws into a fierce grimace. Hold the tense facial expression for 10 seconds. Notice what happens to your breathing. Then release your facial muscles and feel the loose, relaxed expression. (Repeat)
- Move next to your shoulders. Pull your shoulders up toward your ears, tightening your muscles so your shoulders are as high as possible. Feel the tension in your upper back and neck. Hold this scrunched up

posture for 10 seconds. Notice how the rest of your body responds. Then push your shoulders down and back and release the tension. Breathe deeply and relax your shoulders further. (Repeat)

- Focus next on your arms and hands. Flex the muscles of your arms as if you were about to punch someone, clenching your hands into tight fists. Hold for 10 seconds. Notice how you feel and what happens to your breath. Then release the tension and relax your arms and hands, loosening and lengthening each muscle fiber. Feel the tension drain out of the tips of your fingers. Breathe deeply. (Repeat)
- If your mind wanders, gently refocus your attention on your body and breathing.

This technique, called progressive relaxation, helps you to feel the difference between tense, tight postures and loose, relaxed ones. It is impossible to be tense and relaxed at the same time. You're also training your mind to return to a single point of focus, which will help you when you feel overwhelmed by emotional situations.

Studies show regular meditation decreases anxiety and depression, and reduces the physical signs of stress, including high blood pressure, stress hormones and insomnia. These gains aren't just short term perks—meditation retrains the body's response to stress. It also makes you less likely to think negative thoughts about yourself after a difficult task, which means you'll have more mental energy to devote to solving problems because you aren't busy beating yourself up.

Meditation can be combined with other techniques (like yoga) to get added benefits. Take a class or use a DVD to get started.

30. Rethink the Past

Long after a drama subsides, it is helpful to revisit what happened and brainstorm ways to do better next time. Do this alone or with your kids, if they're old enough. Write your thoughts on a big piece of paper or in your journal. Answer questions like these:

- How did you feel? (Be specific.)
- What triggered your feelings?
- Was there a tipping point, when things went from bad to worse? If so, what was it?
- Did personal or situational factors amplify your feelings? How so? Describe the context.
- How did you handle the situation well?
- How did you handle it poorly?
- Was there a turning point, when things went from bad to better? If so, what was it?
- What can you do to prevent the situation from recurring?
- What did you learn about yourself and others?
- How will you act differently next time?

Reflection is a critical part of the learning process. Without it, we're doomed to repeat old patterns of behavior—even though we don't get the results we wanted. A post-meltdown analysis allows you to see this event in the context of other similar events, and notice possible responses that didn't come to mind in the heat of the moment. Lessons learned are easily forgotten if you don't reflect, make connections and consolidate new knowledge.

If you're including the kids in a post-meltdown pow-wow, scale back the questions. Stick with simple prompts like "How did you feel?," "How did you behave?," and "What made you feel better?" Let kids answer completely before sharing your thoughts. What matters is that they think through the experience and make sense of it independently. Offer comments only to clarify and extend their learning.

31. Confront False Beliefs

Intense anxiety or anger often reflect the story we're telling ourselves about a situation or experience, rather than reality. For instance, you might be frustrated that your daughter spilled your coffee all over your desk, soaking your papers and just missing the laptop. But you probably wouldn't be crazy-angry unless you told yourself something like this:

- "I could have lost all the work I did in the last 6 weeks!"
- "No one respects my stuff."
- "It's impossible to for me to get anything done with the kids around."

Bottom line: The issues that really bother you run deeper than the coffee seeping into your desk drawer.

When you feel inklings of fear or anger, ask yourself, "What story am I telling myself about this?" Actively question the truthfulness of your own self-talk. This will help you to expose your interpretations for what they are: wrongheaded, limiting or overblown. Once you confront your false beliefs head-on, you can move forward and solve underlying problems so they don't recur. Put a lock on the office door. Set up a daily automatic hard-drive backup. Schedule your work at a time when the kids are asleep or at school.

After you fix the situation, revise your self-statements so they match reality. Observations like these remind you that your experience is open to a new interpretation.

- "I was lucky that the coffee missed my laptop!"
- "My daughter wants to be just like mommy."
- "I'm taking a risk letting kids in my office."
- "I'm asking a lot of everyone when I try to work and supervise the kids at the same time."

Writing pessimistic and optimistic interpretations side-by-side may help you substitute helpful statements for harmful ones.

32. Affirm your Goodness

When you are feeling low, you may re-hash your mistakes or apply negative labels to yourself. Tweets with the hash tag #momfail range from small slipups like forgetting tooth fairy duty to gigantic missteps like lying about the identity of a child's father.

Resist labeling yourself as lazy, stupid, bad or failing, even when you are really down on yourself. Negative words trap you with feelings of despair and prevent you from changing your behavior for the better.

Answer your inner critic with positive statements about yourself, such as:

- "I am a loving mother."
- "I am doing my best."
- "I can meet my child's needs."
- "I am patient and kind."
- "My child is a precious gift."
- "I enjoy time with my kids."
- "I make the best of every day."
- "I see the good in myself and others."
- "I make amends for my mistakes."

Post these affirmations in visible locations or use a desired belief as your Facebook password. Self-affirming messages can get pre-empt negative self-talk and remind you to stay centered.

33. Forgive Yourself

Self-forgiveness is more than just sitting around waiting to feel better or to forget what you did or didn't do. It must be intentional. Here are three ways to actively forgive yourself:

Reflect compassion. Stand in front of a mirror and talk to yourself in the same gentle tone you'd use with your very best friend. Say, "I know you feel bad about what happened. It hurts me to see you mess up. I forgive you and I know you will do better next time." Communicate the same kind of acceptance and love you'd express to your kids when they make mistakes.

Put it on paper. Write note or letter to yourself extending forgiveness for specific errors. It isn't enough to forgive yourself for being human and fallible. Write, "I forgive myself for losing my temper when the kids painted the dining room walls with spaghetti sauce," then let go of your guilt and self-loathing. One bad outburst does not make you a bad mother. End your letter with a sentence affirming your goodness as a person and as a parent (see technique #32 for affirmations).

Give yourself a hug. Physical touch sends powerful soothing signals to the brain, and bypasses the rational self-critic altogether. If you feel silly hugging yourself, ask your child, partner or pet for a big, warm hug.

Talking about forgiveness is easy. Doing it is hard. Our hearts and minds tend to hold on to the wrongs we've committed. You may feel you need to be punished or that you can't undo what's been done. Although you can't rewrite the past, you can create a different future, and forgiving yourself is the first step in doing so. Actively expressing forgiveness in words or in writing helps you to rethink your attitudes and opens you up to the possibility of revising your behavior. Forgiveness lets you greet the future with optimism and a plan of action.

Your self-compassion session can easily be derailed by self-deprecating thoughts or continued self-punishment. Practice your best detachment skills and put your own inner critic in her place. Tell her she's not the boss of you and that you choose not to accept her destructive comments. Keep at it until you get to a healthy, positive place.

Section Five Recap

Connection, reflection and mindfulness help moms nurture their own emotional well-being. Get a deeper awareness of your feelings and grow from your mistakes with these techniques:

- Find a village
- Make "me" time and space
- Treat yourself
- Rethink the past
- Confront false beliefs
- Affirm your goodness
- Forgive yourself

Practicing these techniques will allow you to approach emotional experiences from a healthy, positive frame of mind.

About the Author

Heidi Smith Luedtke, Ph.D., is the psychologist next door. She received her doctorate in Personality and Social Ecology from the University of Illinois at Urbana-Champaign, where she studied under Ed Diener, an internationally acclaimed happiness expert and one of the founding fathers of positive psychology. Heidi's scholarly work on personality, emotion and coping has appeared in top peer-reviewed journals and edited books. She was Associate Professor of Behavioral Sciences and Leadership at the United States Air Force Academy in Colorado Springs, Colorado, before leaving full-time academic work to marry her best friend and start a family.

Today, Dr. Smith Luedtke is a work-from-home freelance writer whose articles have appeared in more than 80 magazines, including *Parents*, *Pregnancy & Newborn*, *Massage and Bodywork*, *IDEA Fitness Journal*, and *Costco Connection*. She's also a regular contributor to *Military Spouse* magazine, and to a number of regional parenting publications, including *San Diego Family*, *Treasure Coast Parenting*, *Calgary's Child*, and

Western New York Family. In all that she writes, Heidi's goal is to help real people with real problems use psychology to achieve personal growth, healthy relationships, and parenting success.

Acknowledgments

This book would not have been possible without the inspiration, steady encouragement and sage advice of my writing coach and mentor, Christina Katz. I treasure her gentle guidance, technical expertise and dedication to others' success. Simply put: You rock, Christina!

My children, Carson and Avery, give me opportunities to test detachment parenting principles every day. They forgive me when I am a less-than-perfect mother (which is almost every day at 4 p.m.) and quickly let go of bad feelings so we can reconnect and move on. Their generous smiles, hugs and snuggles make me feel like the luckiest mom in the world. Little Boot and Ave-Babe: You stole my heart and gave it back to me one sloppy kiss at a time.

My best friend and husband, Chris, has always supported my home-grown writing career, even when it meant that dinner was leftovers and date night would be delayed until after I met a deadline. He steps in to handle kid drama when I need to catch my breath and boosts my confidence when self-doubt messes with my mojo. I'm especially grateful for his upbeat and sometimes silly attitude. Chris: You make me laugh when I feel like crying.

Finally, I want to thank my parents for their (mostly) patient guidance—I know I wasn't an easygoing kid. You taught me to work hard, roll with the punches, and finish what I start. Whether you knew it or not, you instilled a belief that I could do anything I set my mind to, simply because you never said that I couldn't. Mom and Dad: Thank you for giving me endless opportunities. No kid could ask for more.

Printed in Great Britain
by Amazon